THE TASTE OF STEEL

THE SMELL OF SNOW

Pia Tafdrup was born in 1952 in Copenhagen. She has published over 20 books in Danish since her first collection appeared in 1981, and her work has been translated into many languages. Her fourth collection, *Spring Tide*, was published in English by Forest in 1989. In 1991 she published a celebrated statement of her poetics, *Walking Over Water*. She received the 1999 Nordic Council Literature Prize – Scandinavia's most prestigious literary award – for *Queen's Gate*, which was published in David McDuff's English translation by Bloodaxe in 2001. Also in 2001, she was appointed a Knight of the Order of Dannebrog, and in 2006 she received the Nordic Prize from the Swedish Academy.

Most of Pia Tafdrup's poetry collections have been linked by themes, including *The Salamander Quartet* (2002–2012). Written over ten years, its first two parts were *The Whales in Paris* and *Tarkovsky's Horses*, translated by David McDuff and published by Bloodaxe in 2010 as *Tarkovsky's Horses and other poems*. This was followed in 2015 by *Salamander Sun and other poems*, McDuff's translation of *The Migrant Bird's Compass* and *Salamander Sun*, the third and fourth parts of the quartet.

The first two collections in Pia Tafdrup's new series of books focussing on the human senses are *The Taste of Steel* and *The Smell of Snow*, published as one volume in David McDuff's translation by Bloodaxe in 2021.

THE TASTE OF STEEL

—

THE SMELL OF SNOW

PIA TAFDRUP

TRANSLATED BY DAVID McDUFF

BLOODAXE BOOKS

Smagen af stål [The taste of steel]: © Pia Tafdrup & Gyldendal, Copenhagen, 2014. *Lugten af sne* [The smell of snow]: © Pia Tafdrup & Gyldendal, Copenhagen, 2016. Published by agreement with Gyldendal Group Agency. Translation copyright © David McDuff 2021.

ISBN: 978 1 78037 504 5

First published 2021 by
Bloodaxe Books Ltd,
Eastburn,
South Park,
Hexham,
Northumberland NE46 1BS

Supported using public funding by
**ARTS COUNCIL
ENGLAND**

www.bloodaxebooks.com
For further information about Bloodaxe titles
please visit our website and join our mailing list
or write to the above address for a catalogue.

DANISH ARTS FOUNDATION

Thanks are due to the Danish Arts Foundation
for their grant towards translation costs of this book.

Danish Arts
Foundation

Cover design: Neil Astley & Pamela Robertson-Pearce.

Printed in Great Britain by Bell & Bain Limited, Glasgow, Scotland, on
acid-free paper sourced from mills with FSC chain of custody certification.

CONTENTS

THE SMELL OF SNOW

THE TASTE OF STEEL

Future cycle

To the sound of clouds
the water gives nourishment to the tree
that is food for the fire
that shapes the earth, from where
metal comes; that again

like a catalyst
produces water,

but the water also extinguishes fire,
that melts metal,
that destroys trees
that again destroys earth
to the sound of clouds.

I

No return

Stages on life's way

Your lover, who broke
the sugar bowl,
I am gradually quite indifferent about.
The hate doesn't vibrate any more
at having seen you

dead drunk with infatuation, but
the sugar bowl
I inherited from my mother's mother,
it's still missing
every time I put my hand

in the cupboard, and Søren Kierkegaard's
Stages on Life's Way, which I was
reading, she has spilled coffee on,
just two pieces in the mosaic

of disasters she has loudly
caused in what with steely resolve
I thought was *my* home.

In eternal pursuit

Your gaze scans every room we enter,
it scours the distance when we walk side by side,
your absent inner being, your gaze
I cannot catch, it's in eternal pursuit.

We have each gone in our own direction,
both paths lead to the same point,
both of us sought to turn nothing into something,

dived into dreams in search of the fairytale,
would willingly have loved what we didn't find
in a world of abundance,
while what we found was hard to love,

until the day when even what we found
abruptly disappears for us
and we arrive at a loss,
unreadable as the black holes in the universe,
burning with same storm
that makes us open our eyes wide,

stand like a child
on a pebble in frost and sun
with the fish-hook bored into his finger.

Unposted letter

I dream that my pen
is an axe, I write you
a letter, but the mailbox is out of use,
the postman has gone home,
the post office was long ago converted
into a supermarket filled
with butcher's goods.

In the letter I philosophise about how
misunderstandings happen, even
when we talk with glass-clear voices
swirling inverted between walls of houses down
the street. When I say one thing,
you make ideas of something else,
when you say something, I see only
the pictures *I* form, you say,

we nod, but are, it turns out, cruelly mistaken,
say *yes, yes,*
think we understand each other at last,
yet make the other
quiver white with anger.

I tried to move into
the world, but it spat me out,
as though it didn't like the taste or
was resisting with all its might.

I write with the desire to take part,
not simply pass by without pain, am ready
to take a risk,
though I don't remember having lived even one day
in complete security.

I dream that my pen
is an axe, I write the world, as it writes me,
the colour red
explodes,
write, not so the world will make sense,
merely with an irrational hope
of hacking my way into it, hallo!

Winter blood

'You terrorise me with life,'
you say

and hurl me outside myself
for a moment.

Silence hammers steel,
forges it layer by layer to a Damascus knife,

The words cut dark red,
radiate in the flesh.

'And you terrorise me with death,'
I say

without being able to draw air.

Shiny sharpened sun chill,
flames of fever through the air.

Not even in museums is there peace

I play dead,
so you won't hurt me,
you introduce rules of behaviour
that block my manoeuvres. Thus

for a time together we survive
threats and annihilation.

Museums display daggers, swords
and other weapons, specimens
from many eras, a rich
variation from culture to culture.

In the absence of words
poisoned arrows sing through the air,
but behind the arrows' decoration
the idea is the same: peace
is pauses between wars.

This I understand with a time delay
like a shock to the solar plexus one day
in July's salt sun.

Only the night's defenceless dream
of an embrace, hard and tender,
bears me through the naked day.

II

Meditation

Stopping at the sight of swans

A flock of swans on the water floats in light,
rocked forward by a breeze
that ruffles the lake in the middle of town.

The salt of your words
so unexpectedly rubbed into my wound.

The swans depart in a swoop across the lake,
rise all of a sudden,
take off heavily in a gathered flock.

What powers want the birds to go up
above the water's surface, when they have a lake
of fish-shoals, galaxies of green seaweed?

The wound knows the pain, knows
the fear of death.

A feverish vision of feathers
spreads in a fan of panic
above the rooftops that dazzle in the sun. A rush

of swans through the air
leaving the earth in a silence
so resonant that our souls wander
wildly among one another. And

what do our souls *want*, when they fly up
from our dead bodies,
our drowned dreams.

Plenty of time

Because they can't switch track up north
no train can be on time today,
thousands of people are late, but I
am on a train that was earlier delayed,
and by chance gain time.

I get off, walk down into the viaduct, listen to a band
of young girls, they play and sing, their blood
resounds like echoes in the tunnel,
while ton-weight trains
rumble past on the rails overhead.

To have plenty of time is what I need
to save myself.
It won't take much in the calendar before
my soul keels over,
daily it demands its dose of infinity.

I need to look at the trees far away, look up
now and then while I work, see
the branches move like a sweeping heart in the light, see
birds land in the treetops and fly away again.

I need time to forget time, time
to let time melt glacially.
Free time is plenty of time as long as anyone wants me for anything.

I go up the stairs now, inhale the odours here,
taste the afternoon's late light,
don't guide my steps towards the agreed address, I roam about
in the streets of the city that grows the further I go,
and behind whose walls in the warm night
hear those who can't sleep from sheer love.

Taste

Taste of sharp winds, taste of gale, of hail
and blows of oblivion, of dark of winter steel, taste
of the body's salt, of dry tears, taste of fear,
of sleeplessness long after midnight, taste of stone,
of chill flint, granite, like taste of the fear of being parted

taste of tyres on highways, taste of shiny trains,
metal snakes hunt silently through forests, taste
of ferries, hulls sliding out of their berths, taste of planes
taking off, sounds disappearing, taste of melancholy,

taste of seed and rain, of one's own language, of new words,
of tradition, of migrant birds' caress,
of Kierkegaard's thoughts, Hans Christian Andersen's fairy tales,
taste of the Kattegat and Skagerrak, of the Sound and the Baltic Sea,
taste of dialects, tap water and freedom of speech,

taste of the seasons' and the light's changing, taste of oak and beech,
of elm and maple, linden and lime, of a straw
twiddled between teeth, taste
of silent smiles, of Danish glottal, sound of vowels,
of laughter, of regret, taste of ambiguity's edge,

taste of centre and periphery, of the space in
between, over which the spider spins
her web, taste of dew in grass, taste
of the unarticulated, what is only on the way,
the indefinable taste of a secret,

taste of fever, taste of restlessness, the taste of biting
the sour berries in midday sun as a child,
the taste of memory, that can still make the saliva
leap, taste of sun, of ice and snow crystals' light,

taste of squandered life, taste of a newly invented day,
the tongue follows lines in an arabesque,
taste of raw milk, not drops of an eternity,
taste of a farewell kiss, the final words,
of dizziness at sea and sky, the earth's rotation.

Undercurrent

The lake borders on rocks and woods,
Even in the middle of the day a night of metal,
knife edges of sunbeams flicker over the water.

The lake is a gigantic mirror for a stream
of jagged clouds, sheer being,
when the sky drains itself.

Here is captured the fleeting,
the unbounded, the ever
changing.

What is going to die,
by contrast,
brands the mind with glowing iron
when it becomes clear
that death
is approaching,

as the undercurrent in deep lapping
against the bottom of the boat now
signals power of hidden forces,
and the smell of lake water

grows sharp with silt and rot,
while the world shaped by itself
still swims in the universe.

Loneliness

The world is full of names
we have invented,
not in order to burst

one another's eardrums,
or to make the tongue avoid
a void,

but to overcome the loneliness
we have in common,

Even God, who has shaped us
from language,
we have given a name,
and with hands suited for catching snowflakes
or setting butterflies free,

tried to wall Him up in buildings
as architecturally various
as churches, synagogues, mosques,
temples and pagodas,

even though God,
who is born at every moment, it is said,

is the life of the endless deep,
and does not cease His revolt.

III

Off track

Earring

I can't really ask a husband to repair
the earrings I got
from another man.

For hours I have tried myself
to wiggle the little clip in place,
but it still won't take hold
of my ear.

My fingers are at work, my soul
is working. Overtime.

The other man gives me
earrings from a stall in a piazza
in Rome, they are oval, they glow

like a consummated sunset,
but to repair them is also
unthinkable. There is no time

for repair, I could have been
more cautious with that gift.
To make me a present of earrings
was not what the first man would do, it

would never occur to him
to give me earrings
such a long time after the wedding and certainly not
to take me to Rome, but

he is good at repairing things,
for a whole lifetime he has repaired my life,
kept me going with,
but mostly without, earrings.

After frost-white shell of cold

I don't prefer the chirping of the birds
to silence, nor silence
to the chirping of the birds. I like
the wind's gust, the change

between sounds and absence,
of sounds, the lustful chaos of song
each spring,
as well as the state of things afterwards,

when something slowly expands
in all directions, starts to smoulder behind
the night's pulse. Restlessness,
invading longing, a narrow
chink in the hard shell.

To give what cannot be taken,
to take what can only be given,
a single sigh brings it all together.

Japanese cherries

Cherry trees in breathless blossom
like the answer to a winter sky's snow, to echoes of frost.
A plunge down into sweetness,
pull of warm spring.

You stand behind me with your hands
round my shoulders, hold me tight.
Flower-clouds of light and fragrance,
an invisible link between sex and soul.
Your lips on my neck,
when I lean my head back to stare in
to the treetops' glow, the same pink play of colours
as in a sunrise

or a newly healed-up scar.
Your kisses along the neck up
to the ear, an inner snowfall
that summons forth
the dead, who are not granted
season by season to see
the trees, when they spring out.

A breeze rocks the branches in the mild air,
the first blossoms descend
like everything we throw away,
settle on the ground that soon
looks like a sea where a funeral has taken place
in a storm of silence.

Night country

Trunks sway, the leaves
on the thinnest branches
lick the ground in long strokes,
attempt to fly in the wind
over the gravel and the grass, the park
pulsates blindly.

Small stones crunch beneath the feet of the one
who steps into
the domain of lost dreams,
finds something darker than the night's hiding place

in rest, in leaping,
and without words,
hands or birds, only

with a heart
prehistorically thumping against
the tree's trunk of the tree or the earth's unendingness,

far away from a delta
of worries, which in a sleepless rush
attack the brain's cortex.

Fish in the lake rise up
to the surface to see
the moon galvanise the park, before
the rain comes. Heavy rain.

Leaves ease rocked by the droplets,
silver,
tell the smell, sharp as a dagger.

Metal

The strings' vibration
spreads from the guitar's deep bass,
drums in battle with themselves,
tones smack against the ear. Taste
of the rain's strokes
on the tip of the tongue,

the music's metallic shower
on the verge of bone fracture,
torrential rain
on the sun in the body now.

Impossible to seal a waterfall
of tones' steel.
Kaleidoscopic thoughts are set free,
raise the water, loosen the hips' edge,
make the blood rise steeply,
bodies on the stage and in the hall sway in time.

Do I hear my own breathing,
or is it a sum
of the pulses of other listeners,
the rain's colours rinse free
with the blood's flow
in the expanding night.

The bass's friction in every fibre-thread,
light-stroke, light-pulse,
still hoarsely

alive, the bodies lead nowhere else
than here,
where in the semi-darkness I giddily meet your smile.

I know where I have been, not where I am going
under a sky shiny
with lightning.

Bodies without root nets

Not a voice, not a language
a tongue breaks in, drink my name.
No one belongs to anyone,
each heart beats alone in its body.
Between the lips the tongue extends,
an alien flame. Fire

makes the skin prickle everywhere,
the night reflect itself on closed eyelids.
What does the body do, it opens
as when an oar-blade
punctures the black surface of a lake.

What do bodies do without root nets,
like plants shrubs or a tree,
they rise without a trace,
they loosen up, they stretch out
into the water's stream world,
they go swaying, swirling quietly on.

Do we come alive under caresses,
do we radiate, or do we efface one another
when our bodies become one
with the darkness outside,
where stars are thrown to the ground, and we
float, dive and gather the water's deep stream.

Down

Off track. You, I,
in each other's arms.
The sun rises
in the night's vault,
pain-desire, pain-pulse.

Kisses glow against
cheek, neck, chest,
longing bodies
fill the night.
An animal lives
in the brain,
it leaps free.

The sound of a look,
the fragrance in the room.
Find the direction
towards the point
that gathers everything.

As never
I can only,
you only, enter
each other, we,
lips, tongue, sex,
beloved. Down
on our knees. Our places.
Sounds fleeing from our lips
in the dense darkness
dots of light sing,

dance before our eyes.

Our breathing
directs the wind.
The heart beats

as the heart, given oxygen,
the moment's avalanche
of oblivion.
Separate from everything,
sink each into
our own shadow, wander
underground, separate.

IV

Crossroads

Power cut

Suddenly the power goes in the middle of a poem:
Schweigen, wie Gold gekocht, in
verkohlten
Händen,
in the middle of cooking my fish
out there in the kitchen,
the music vanishes, what did I hear in the distance?
The light goes, the TV. In the way that a newly born's

hovering gaze
investigates if the world exists,
everyone in the room looks at one another. Who was here
before I closed the book?

The men with hoarse voices in the bar, people scattered
at the tables. The waiter moves routinely
in the room, serves the fish in the dark,
I recognise it as a fish,
before the light arrives, the music:
you really got me, the TV lady
is back on the screen. In sign language

she gesticulates about air strikes
on civilians, people killed in the queue for bread,
but with only a few strokes in the air the power is gone again,
the chain reaction broken.
A regular customer enters from the street on a direct course
for the bar in the darkness, gets his drink
without ordering it.

We talk to the men in the bar over
the tables of bread-baskets and wine,
embarrassed to have only now

discovered the world, as though we are suddenly
noticing heart and lungs. The light

is back, the sign lady on TV,
soundless hands in the air as before,
but at the tables and in the bar the mood is high,
they laugh, the men, while the music plays
you really got me going.

Pont Neuf

While the streets shine white in the snow's brilliance
and night after night the grown-ups
talk with friends about enemies,

a little girl sleeps her winter sleep
with both arms over her head
like wings,

begins a journey from
the stone age of dreams. Wakes

from her torpor with the earliest
budding trees along the Seine one day in March.

Takes the first steps of her life
in the smallest size of shoes in the sunshine on Pont Neuf,
stumbles, but is lifted at once,
a whole family seizes hold.

Steers her arms in the air,
gurgles and calls forth
laughter from anyone
who may have forgotten

the victory it is
to move upright. Soon ready
to hurry for the bus, click
her tongue, dance like a spark
from the fire, get lost
in a maze of sex and violence,
make friends and enemies.

A bridge in light,
a river swirling dark
with many dead.

The bridge over the river, the river's flow
under the bridge, a crossroads
of light and shadow.

Boats sail. Clouds fly across the sky
with signature of clouds, without goodbyes.

Daily choice

Here, where the distant sky feels quite near
out on the narrow balcony
in the wind, one can

standing like a tensed string
choose either to throw oneself

down on the pavement,
or as far as the eye can see, look
out into the horizon from sunrise
to sunset.

The child in the cradle clutches
the grown-up's finger,
does not release her grip.

At night, when the city lights,
like the reflection from a sea on fire,
wash into the parlour over the black lacquer table,
it is hard to refrain from

stepping out on the balcony, bathing in a light-flood
of flashing white,
signal red and siren coloured blue.

As a safeguard against the pull of the depths an easily
forceable grid has been set up.
Only the vertical view
down

makes the letters smell of blood.
Love is hands that open, everything
may be there or be lost abruptly.

The pets and their people

The city is weightless in suddenly hot air,
a spring day
when lovers, if they are not expecting a child,
are paralysed by a puppy.

The blood freezes in my heart at the sight of
a half-stunned creature. It is lifted
out of its cage in the store's half darkness, where I,
on the way down to buy bread,

missing my cat in Copenhagen,
have looked in
to greet its fellow felines.

The puppy lays its head sleepily against
the woman's shoulder, the cars are inaudible,
voices from the outside are gone.

A warm and unfamiliar smell
belongs to the two of them, now that the three
are soon in one another's power.

The man is handed the creature and its
uncertain upbringing, instantly transfixed
by the woman's gaze.

The young couple don't speak, but visibly to me
their hopes flow
together while both caress the puppy.

It will not go back to its cage,
is carried home to the bowl and the basket, without
yet having shown its true canine nature.

Time and space

Roadside bombs under a sectioned sky,
the earth is the same, it is only borders, limits
that are perceptibly or imperceptibly changed.

That face that looks at me from the mirror's surface
is changing year after year beyond recognition and is
recognised none the less.

I cannot wake up and see
myself as a child, only
where I find myself at this moment.

The language we speak is not quite
the same as before,
sound and meaning have shifted,

like a restless ocean,
like the architecture of clouds
in continuous transformation.

Time, it is called, but I sense space.
That the past exists osmotically here,
that all are present, the living and the dead.

Life is a continuous state of emergency,
nothing comes back, everything
comes back different.

Behind my eyes are souls from before,
just as present as you and I
forever here and now.

V

War

The darkness machine

The child should be running around
in the sun,
it should be playing, not
struck in the back by a bullet, not

paralysed from the waist down
by a war
whose shiny metal
penetrates the sound of the words
with the grey taint of vengeance,

and whose conflicts
hound the heart, settle
like moon-coloured scars
on a whole generation.

Razed city

A bomb has fallen and made heaven deaf,
a district has turned into ruins.

The daily praxis is not possible here,
where the impossible has taken place,
it dissolves, exists only as dream pictures now.

The boy's gaze is directed down,
the father also looks at the ground,
the boy huddles on his arm.

Everyone is staring at the piles of stone,
which before were tall buildings in the city centre.

Where can people find one another?
In which collapsed house
on which street?

The only fixed point
is uncertainty, anxiety,
the open ground.

The words have grown smaller, too small
for this ragnarök, for blood and chaos.

The horror continues
palely, grows like lost reason.

The journalist's question

Ask him why he sits in the smell of cordite
and dust from the rubble in the street. Why
flies crawl over his neck and nape. Why
he sweats so heavily in the white light.

Ask him if he knows why he is
alone there, if he wants to talk to someone, with whom.
Or if he prefers to listen to the barking of the dogs
and the traffic in the almost empty street.

Ask him if no houses recognise him,
if there are no places to visit.
Ask him why he sits with
the empty cup in his hand.

Ask him why he still
holds his head high,
as if the city can't do without him.
Ask him if he has all his senses intact.

Ask him why the sky is the colour of mourning,
and his eyes are as black as the night.
If he is waiting for a miracle.
Ask him why his life is a question.

Spring's grave

Don't sleep,
don't let your dreams
hide the sight of the massacre.

A polite young man
reflects himself in hatred and revenge,
wants to bring a country to its knees,
follows the sun as a farewell, life
to kill.

The eyes slowly get used
to the darkness, but only
to stare into
a larger dark, stare oneself blind
at the questions of an enigma.

Wash the blood away, send small coffins.

Thoughts move about restlessly,
need rises
like the water at high tide.

A well's depth of mourning,
prayer that hope
can take root in the impossible.

But only send small coffins.

A before and an after

There's a difference in the body when it carries weapons
and when it doesn't,
there's a difference whether I have physically and mentally
trained myself
to handle weapons or not.

Am I a belligerent creature, or do I go around
without weapons, full of trust?
Am I one who kills, or one
who breathes against the steel's burning frost
while the sun is growing,
blood-open?

The tongue is rough. Between the lips no words.
Metal wedges its way
into the flesh or bores into
the heart, where the planets of the night go orbiting
to throw light on the dreams in the brain's prehistoric darkness.

View from space

From the sixth planet from the Sun in our solar system,
where the Cassini space probe
trains its camera lens on the Earth, it's visible merely

as a small, white dot.

That's where I live far away, that's where my cat today
has seen a deer for the first time,
that's where the cat probably thought
it had landed on an alien planet.

In NASA's image the Earth is photographed from just
ten times the distance
from the Earth to the Sun. I am close to
Saturn and its rings of stone and ice,

a gigantic silence reigns here.

I see the Earth from outer space,
see the bright glowing dot.
That's where I live, that's where we live,
that's where we live as if we were the centre
of the universe.

That's where butterflies hover over the grass,
that's where we ceaselessly produce
more weapons, practise battle tactics,
turn our everyday lives into a night of hell,

that's where I obliterate, that's where I'm annihilated.

VI

Waiting

Chink

Wake with the autumn's gale,
before autumn arrives.
A fierce wind
scurries among the treetops,

lie stretched out in a bed
some place on earth where
no one puts their arms around me.

A window is thrust open
to the night's cold, the lungs
breathe in raw air,
the heart's beat in the room facing north.

The reflex of one's breathing
is set on the future
but not assured,

pass

an invisible border, listen to
the metal in stone,
the metal deep in the earth,

the meridian centre,
to thousands of heartbeats.
Slowly life takes
the life from us.

A squirrel bids welcome

If I promise not to take a single nut,
says the gaze from the creature
which, standing upright on its hind legs with white belly
and a very long tail hanging out
over a branch in a spruce tree,
has a long look at me,

is it all right
if I settle down here.

The red squirrel moves again
like zigzag lightning
between trees and bushes in the garden it inhabits.

I tear handfuls of bindweed
up from the hedge of wild roses on a burning day in August,
then sit with a glass of water
in the dry sun
on a chair with pen and notepad,

hear the squirrel up from a bush
loudly crack nut after nut,

which I would like,
but refrain from picking
instead gnawing my way in
to the alphabet letter by letter,
interrupted only by the creature, when with tail as a rudder
it steers the metre-long leaps
horizontally from tree to tree,
as though it had opened a motorway
with no traffic rules on its territory.

Despair drinks fire

The heat from the heart of Europe
lands in Denmark late in October.
the leaves glow in the terrain, before
they descend from the trees.

In Italy a man sets himself on fire,
because he has no work,
but seven children to support.

A grown man
becomes a fragile boy,
a woman a girl again.

Rays of sun make the dew glow like a veil,
the birds sing or pull up worms
from the wet soil.
A squirrel leaps from a hawthorn
to the grass, finds food for its cache,

dashes around among fallen leaves,
undisturbed by chattering magpies
and humans' problems
in feeding their family.

One doesn't give the children food
by blazing up like a torch.

Fear has bored its way
into the man's breast, and heaven has got lost.
The pain is his alone, wordless,
sets other souls on fire.

Life with pigeons

From the top of a half-withered birch
two pigeons sail through the mild autumn air,
settle down not far from me.
My mother's pigeons, fried
golden and served in a powerful sauce
of lead shot and guilt for us

and the hunter, my father.
Remember the heavy sleep after a meal
of wild game from heaven.

My first impulse: food
on the table, not the dove of peace, not the dove I
sacrificed as a child on my father's field,
where the smoke crept low

over the stubble instead of rising straight up into the air,
as I had heard
it ought to, not the pigeons that give loneliness sound

by cooing each from a tree,
not the pigeons placed on gravestones
or flocks of dusty pigeons in the city's squares,
called flying rats,

nor the pigeons I feed with sunflower seeds
on the sill to entice them
as encouragement for my cat,
who, despite years of incarceration in a city apartment,
with all his instincts intact
teeth chattering with concentration, goes hunting

on the windowsill between books and pot-plants

on the other side of the glass, which from time to time
he forgets is there, when he tries to strike
at her prey, hammers on the pane only
to see another pigeon flap away,

but with a certain time lag
lands safely with members of its own species here in the poem.

Frog

It's not a dead leaf from last year,
carried along by the wind
in the middle of April,

but a common frog,
that has woken up
from hibernation and very deliberately,

as a contrast to my day's
row of procrastinations,
comes in long hops

over the grass to the window that reaches
from floor to ceiling,
so I can follow the year's transformation of light.

Again and again outside the frog
tries to jump up the glass.

I open a pane
above the grey-green warty creature,
look down into the frog's black eye,
when it looks up

and with its long legs
tries further jumps,
as if with all its strength

on this spring day, when heaven reaches
earth, it insists on
bringing the past of tailless amphibians

into my present life
in the stove's warmth here indoors.

VII

Loss

The anonymous part of the churchyard

In the anonymous part of the churchyard
where there are no marked graves
and no gravestones
for the dead,
my mother has bought herself a place
in eternity
near the tree beside my father.

That place no one else shall have,
here my father waits.

In my mind all the fields lie fallow,
the forests have been cut down,
but the sun
still rises and sets,
good morning, good night.
The horses eat out of my hand,
the wind gathers up with the words I seek.

Each in our own flame

Are there any amusing deaths,
said my mother,
when younger, and before
the many visits
to nursing homes, she picked up
the daily paper. Now everyone

around her is dying, love
is supplanted by cremation,
parties replaced by funerals.
The yellowed address book is filled
with crossed-out names.

My mother no longer remembers
what it was like to be married,
the mirror reflects nothing.
It's nine years since my father died,

I remember what it was like
to have a father,
to sing when I played, see
his face, hear his voice.

He turned the worst nightmares
into pure insignificance.
With his presence alone
he could make calm fall
on any room.

He carries my death
in him.
Each in our own flame we must burn to ash.

Porous border

The day begins a new sky
with smoke-coloured clouds, the water glistens grey.
The taste of the kiss from the farmhand's son
has been washed away with the whole of Lake Esrum.

My childhood place no longer exists
as I knew it. Three
of the farm's four wings burned
to the ground, others built over,
the garden split up
into parcels. Houses are close together,
where before trees grew that cast

long shadows. My sleep
pursues a place that is a different one today,
my sleep burns down the dream
like the stalls with the animals.

Eggs have been thrust from my thighs,
milk has left my breast.

Like a dog on the road
memories run up to me,
the way my mother grabs hold
of things that happened long ago and clings on.

My mother is in constant change,
cells are alive, cells break down,
but the voice is her voice, the smell her smell,
the soul has its own integrity.
When she asks about what happened once,
I nearly cease to exist, don't know who
is cracking and who is intact.

I'm her child playing on the floor while
the sun shines through the rain,
her young daughter, who is flirting with a man
she wanted to poison,
her grown-up daughter who has just had her children.

The world's complexity my mother
has resigned herself to,
the most recent years of my life are lost in mist.

I come to visit,
open my bag, lend her books from my bookshelf,
which she reads and forgets again,
the light falls obliquely into the parlour, my mother
sees me, but at once sinks into
echo chambers of the past.

We walk from the garden down the gravel road
to Lake Esrum, I'm three or four years old,
her hand is warm as now,
the water flashes under the sky. Together we find
mushrooms in the meadow, fill a basket.

Inside, the animals are burning, frenetic fire,
my breathing stops.
What I am telling my mother doesn't listen to,
just likes that I'm talking, that *someone* is talking,
that there's *someone* in her parlour, I,
my sister or my brother.
The knife of fire in the heart twists round

and round,
her love has taken root in what
isn't here.

The clock shows nothing,
who's disappearing for whom,

the earth is so far away.

A display case filled with night

Slowly the darkness rises,
the wind moves the trees in one
and the same place as what
has happened in the course of the years, circles around me.

On the table under the lamp lies the cat, too old
to hear. It sits up, looks out,
doesn't pick up the bird's song as I do, probably
sees something I can't make out

in the twilight that grows with these lines to
a denser darkness where things
disappear like greetings that came once,
like missing letters and calls.
Quiet at last, and yet

tiny sounds to register, the ones
that can't be heard when there is noise,
the evening's last blackbird notes, a faint
creaking in the house, the wind in the chimney's channel.
The cat arches its back, lies back down on the same spot,
purrs.
The trees are indistinguishable from one another, the grass can't be seen,
the darkness closes, a display case filled with night.

The gaze turns inwards. Another space
opens, impossible to demarcate, but filled
with images that pursue me,
breed like dreams from a mountain mass,
when the night shines pupil-black.

What the thoughts wander subterraneanly after,
they don't always find, but something else leaps out

metal-hard or fever-fragile,
a numeric code burned into the skin, a heart in clay,
facial muscles rigidly fixed, creatures
frozen still in ice.

The images strike home like people's judgment,
they glow in the night like the countdown to death
through the cells' seismographic behaviour,
sharpen the days, make visible
history's progress
amidst the chronology,
when the spine straightens in extreme attentiveness
far down from a root system
up to the frozen sparks which in constant transformation
swirl behind the brain's shell.

On the other side

The sky bright blue, the birds invent the spring now,
great tits, chaffinches, blackbirds accompanied
by magpies and pigeons. It's blowing in gusts
on the path between birches and pines,
where you ring me up, my friend.

You speak with tears in your voice,
but I am happy about a sentence
I have written on the first mild day of the year.
The world has not gone under. We are still
in the passage,

planets float through space,
we draw breath, talk, while your mother
is on the other side of the life
where oxygen can reach the lungs.

Pictures of her fill you,
behind closed eyes you see
ceaselessly more, and in your dreams she speaks.
Her body is still here,
frost still, the flesh
where all kinds of pain lived.

The corpse has not entered the earth, it exists,
but the pain is gone,
the voice, the shine of the eyes.
What direction does a soul seek
with voice and shine of eyes,

does it take up residence
in us, or seek it further away?
From earth we have come, in earth
we shall bury the corpse, but down there
the soul will hardly venture.

Greeting from the deceased

Soundless in the grass. Forwards.
The roe deer stops a few metres in front of me
like a greeting from the deceased.

A deer she took up residence in
comes now and eats from the pile of seeds
I have put out
for the birds in the early morning sun.

Another deer follows her, also eats
the seeds in the grass.
The birds in the trees see her, I
see her, recognise in the deer her gaze,
when it looks up at me,
feel her presence in the heart's region.

Did not get to say goodbye,
but now she is here the day after her death.
From one country to another she has come,
from one life to another,

I sit quite still, let the creatures eat.

Snow flowers

The snow has settled on the branches, filled
the empty birds' nests in trees and bushes along
roads that all lead to the church.
The March sun dazzles, the snow on the ground dazzles,
shadows fall where we walk,
flocks of crows circle high up above us.

The cold in the church, the cold round our feet, silence
swirls giddily in the vaulted space,
where no sounds from outside
penetrate.
Having to lose is what we can't make ourselves ready for.

The dead woman
we have come to bury is not here. No tracks
lead anywhere.
An invisible frontier is passed, a part
of our life is gone,
a chapter of Europe's history over.

We must bury the body she left behind,
she herself continued,
though we see her in the open coffin, give thanks for
what we received.

We see the dead woman,
see her dressed in travel clothes, see the dead woman
with mouth closed and lips pressed together,
though in life she always laughed and talked,
muscles robbed of movement, skin like stone.

There was a time when it was to us
she laughed and talked.

The loss we must all bear, it
does not make it any less hard.

We see and don't understand. We are present here
and don't understand.

We lay flowers, stand
in the smell of incense with lighted candles.
Except that her head is not tilted,
the dead woman resembles
the image of the Virgin Mary in the icon
that is placed in the open coffin.

The funeral is
for the living, the dead woman's soul
has already gone.
Several days ago it vanished for us.

Dear soul,
we bury your body, but you are free.

The language we speak is not the same as before,
the snow falls into me,
snow flowers drift cold in the blood.
We look and look at the dead woman.
The sight of her face is imprinted
forever, the wax candles are burning down.

Now it is us. Now loneliness shines.
Star-visited night,
multiplied arrival,
frost-lit fields, ice-bound soil,
loss burns itself into the mind,
a strange and unfamiliar freedom.

Residue

Empty room after room, basement and attic,
open secret places, throw things away,
carry out piles of rubbish, dig blindly
in the darkness of closets for armfuls of clothes,
sling them into trash bags, press them down
with half-closed eyes, remove, clear up,
increase one's pulse rate, step out
of the dead person's
shadow,

let buyers painlessly
collect the last loads, clear out,
reveal squares of damp and dirt,
ferry furniture and boxes through corridors,
through steel lift doors, drive quickly away.

Or stand with object after object,
twist and turn it in the light,
sort, place in neat stacks,
wrap the most valuable in newspaper,
let the day's news enshroud
bowls, pots and glasses,
make presents of things to this relative and that,
dwell on one memory and the next,
be burned by sudden cold, lose oneself
in scents and imprints, continue
to water the plants,
gradually bring chairs and tables home,
letters, photos and other belongings,
to become a part of oneself
by being a part
of the dead person,

feel the pulsing blood
and at least five senses,
but not forget that one day
one will also
be a liberating memory for others.

Threshold

An engine is turned off, I hear the wind,
hear a myriad birds very close.
In the sun storksbill are popping out, blue
as the sky above me,

it is almost possible to see them open
flower by flower in the heat. A jerk
in the crowns of the birches, each leaf

eavesdrops on itself and the other leaves, partakes
of a common effervescence.
In the midst of a steel-cool touch of breeze
I realise that I dreamed about my father
last night, but can't remember what.

An earwig that doesn't know
it's an earwig
crawls crystal-shining in the sun
over the step in the open doorway, while I

find no entrance to my own dream,
which in relation to sleep's circumference
seems unending.

What did my father want?
He exists inside me, after all,
can't choose to be gone,

he exists far over the years' loss
of boundaries, he is here
as himself, but brings something with him,

something I cannot determine.
New shoots of vegetative wisdom
grow with the summer.

VIII

Words

Crime scene

A little of the snow that fell so abundantly
last year
I send away with the wind and my thoughts
to the park in December, which now
in eleven degrees sprouts as in February.

If the cold comes once again,
it doesn't mean murder
of a sprout that with the same name
as the years before has risen up

above the ground in the sun's glow.
It waits like words in the middle of a sentence
that doesn't know how
to go on, but one day

nevertheless finds its end,
planted in a poem because the author under cover
of darkness returns to her crime scene here.

No different than when an old lover
is visited so faithfully in the dreams
that not for one second have doubted in him,
that one day again he would
stand at the door wearing new shoes.

Mother tongue

I burst into loud laughter
in my mother tongue,

am understood in another country,
my friends laugh back
in their language.

I cry
in my mother tongue,

am understood in another country,
comforted by arms
that cradle me.

Word and soul

The words in the book penetrate an armour.
What I read burns like a field
of ice and blood,
is tattooed in without deaf pain,

penetrates the mind.

How do letters and soul meet,
thought and soul?
How does the soul find meaning in words

which may have found their way
without the writer knowing from where,
and now across the paper's time

take root in me. Taste them!

The words exist, they
can be retrieved from a place
that is by no means an overgrown wilderness.

There is room for more words,
the space in the brain is
apparently no smaller than the universe.

Searchlight

Is there a meaning in life
in the work of Kafka, Camus, Duras
or in catching and cleaning
a sea-cold fish,

is it in raising one's thumb in the air,
hiking a lift
into the intense unknown,

is it in love in boring into
your arms, kissing my way
from the neck hollow down to your sex,

is it in writing oneself language-awake into
the future with one's questions,
doing yoga, laying tarot cards,
giving birth to a child. Yes,

giving birth to a child and listening to
scales in the mysterious intersections of all languages,
sounds that are fixed as Danish
by filtering others away,

in letting the child be a bridge,
letting it listen and repeat a way
into the world
until the words fall like warm rain,
drops that simply *are*,

like the meaning in *not*
searching for meaning,
and yet finding sense.

Johan Borgen – a ritual

At the start of every morning Johan Borgen took a bath,
groomed himself carefully, dressed
as for a festive occasion, before he wrote,
you saw him on TV long ago taking his morning walk
along the rocky shore in a cold wind,
gulls in the air, shoals of fish in the gray sea.

I do as Johan Borgen did, step out
of sleep's space, begin the day with a bath,
let the water spray and shower skin
hair, nails, a delight
of rays every morning, a rain of light,
but never the same drops.

I wash the wilderness of night away, wash away the sweat,
the collective, the cultural,
sweat of all beings, all destructive thoughts, stand

white and naked on the bath mat, relieved,
without having wept like a mountain,
a cloud of steam fills the room, windows fog up,
water drips from my body.

I take deep breaths,
the world is not old now,
pain absent at this moment
when I focus, land in myself.

The light breaks through, I dress as for a festive occasion,
notice this ordinary day
becoming a special day, sit down at my desk,
let the thoughts wander, the words come, words
I love and struggle with.

I stretch myself out across myself,
below me fly the birds.

Poets

Poets seldom talk seriously together,
they talk in monologues beside one another,
when they really get going
sound most of all like open letters, shipwrecked dreams.

As a rule they loudly tear thorns out of their own flesh,
when they sit round the table with half-empty glasses,
or talk over each other about death,
which approaches with ever greater speed.

They are each assailed so excitedly by language
that for one whirring second they think they've been understood.
The birds don't hear them, they recite the songs of the wind,
their tones drown them out undisturbed.

IX

Paradox

Harvest

It is no longer enough
to pick apples and pears from the trees
or dig metal out of the ground,

now gold and platinum must be harvested
from distant asteroids in the solar system,

mineral mining operations run
high above the stars far out in space.
It is only a foretaste of more,

and we go on,
though we're merely descended from a worm
with mouth and anus in one,

whose system
does not work very differently
from a giddy roundabout.

Separation

The moment I begin to love,
the separation starts,
at least the fear of separation.

The fire grows in the blood,
I can't turn back,
can't remain,

the condition reminds me of the unrest
that sits in my body
when I have slept a sleep,
that does not make me more awake.

My pain is not yours,
and vice versa,
yet it is not impossible
to distinguish your pain from mine,
when I look into your eyes,
and you look into mine.

I throw myself out,
no one can hold me, I simply fall
deeper within myself.

A decision is possible,
it exists in me like a freedom
greater than myself,
but it is mine alone
and therefore a prison.

As long as a pain pierces through
it's not over.

The taste buds wake up

There isn't much that doesn't
taste of anything, broken glass
has a taste, the bread of angels,
paper, unrequited love,
the cry from the throat.

The taste buds are there to enjoy,
to distinguish between fresh and stale,
between sweet and sour, salt and bitter. And umami,
that sets off other tastes.

Taste is more than an electric impulse,
it is the recognition of mother's milk,
my blood, my sweat, my tears and other
chemical molecules, your skin, your sex.

With 10,000 taste buds on the tongue, each with
about 1,000 receptors
taste will not let itself be overcome.
The water I drink tastes of the water of Østerbro,
as wine has a taste of vintage and locality,
which can make it so surprisingly good
that I get lost in streets far from my neighbourhood.

There isn't much that has no
taste of something, broken glass
has a taste, the bread of angels,
paper, requited love,
the cry from the throat.

We are born again

I remember you as the river remembers its flow,
and when I happen to see you again,
I disappear for a moment,
forget to take in air, I shake, get out of breath.

Love doesn't just sit like a brilliant needle
in one's clothes, it is stuck far into
the soul in order to destroy.

The body does not react very differently
in states of sudden panic or anxiety attacks,
the same feeling of unreality,
identical palpitations and fear
of losing control of oneself.

If I don't set myself free
from the love that makes me feel more lonely,
I shatter,

but the river remembers its flow, remembers that light,
which falls by itself between you and me.
Without *that* love I can't live.

I see you,
jump over the wind, the blood courses newly born towards *now*.

Animal smell of light

A tree has toppled over in the storm, it looks
horizontal now
with the roots jerked up.

Earth spurted heavenwards
like a black ejaculation.

Birds sing on unconcerned
from other trees,
as if their tongues
had pulled all the vowels
out of the alphabet.

Often starting over is
a continuation, some leave their lives
so others can sing free.

Killer whales

The water is high behind my walls, presses in,
slowly the walls begin to give way.
The wallpaper cracks, wall and ceiling
have cracks. The pressure is gigantic,
the water will topple in

the moment it breaks through.
On the bed lies a stranded man.
I have got up and huddle in a chair
in a corner by the window with a view of the sea in a room
shaped like a pentagram.

I have seen killer whales fly above the water
in high leaps, outstretched, out-tensed
– hanging in the air –
sovereign and solitary, seen them pierce a hole
with their snouts in the waves' dance floor,
let their enormous bodies follow after with a splash,

as if the water were going to wash over every surface.
One second memory, oblivion the next,
the wind catches the windows, a draught blows in.
I sneeze loudly, the coffee is cold
in the chipped cup.

The sky. The light. The white clouds. The grey ones.
Something wants into this room with all its might.
The roar of the sea. In
to my sleep, into my life.

Through the holes in my skull I feel
something raging and trying to overturn a sorrow-filled mind.
The surf through millions of years,

the whales' primordial force. The walls won't withstand
the pressure, I know.

Wept at the sight of the whales,
these creatures at once heavy and elegant,
fearsome in their strength.
Torpedo-shaped they hurtled away
through an underwater space, into
the wasteland of consciousness.

They exist, live at the same time as I,
rise, fall with metre-high splashing,
deafen me, blind me with their being. Like this
they can lead to anything, give an aftertaste
of the world's beginning, my gaze
suddenly looks around: The world is open,
a breath makes the difference.

Early morning

To pull up the blind
after a pitch black night
with dreams of destruction,
see that it's all there:

the houses, the trees, the birds,
figures walking on the road

in the early morning light
when a blood-coloured rosehip
becomes the centre of the world.

THE SMELL OF SNOW

I

Breathe in, breathe out

Spirit

I breathe in snowy air, breathe in a universe,
the snow falls, dances between trees, dances
under street-lamps' light-cones, the snow has lost the sky,

the snow whirls through space, I breathe in cold,
breathe in purity, the snow is rest for the soul,
thoughts rise up, expand, while each flake seeks

its casual centre in the world, the snowy sky settles
on the earth, something reaches out across the body's limit,
something exists that's greater than I can grasp, merely sense,

the snowy sky settles over my heart,
I breathe in the air that binds
us together, to each other.

Spirit is noticed when it's present, touches
as with a wing tip, a puff of wind, a wave of mist,
leaves its mark of elevation when it suddenly arrives,

spirit is joined to my consciousness, but also
greater than it, spirit can reach the consciousness of all,
it's there between us, we talk together,

understand each other in glimpses, reach into each other's lives,
by means miraculous or barbaric, words are a breathing out and in,
I breathe in the smell of snow, breathe out, breathe in, like you.

Prana

Expand my lungs in a scream from prehistoric times to now,
breathe in ... breathe out ...

I smell my mother: stone, water, cherry blossom,
breathe in ... breathe out ...

I yawn, I hiccup, laugh and cry,
breathe in ... breathe out ...

I eat and drink, sleep quietly,
breathe in ... breathe out ...

I live, understand myself, the air sings,
breathe in ... breathe out ...

I procreate, I give birth, gasp, am beyond myself,
breathe in ... breathe out ...

I am shocked, hurt, I'm paralyzed by fear,
hold my breath ... ... breathe out ...

I inhale the past, air others have exhaled,
breathe in ... breathe out ...

I exhale air that others later will inhale,
breathe in ... breathe out ...

I write, my heart beats, freshly oxygenated blood,
breathe in ... fill my lungs ... breathe out ...

smell life, share the light, the air and the moment
breathe in ... breathe out, dream death –

Fresh snow

I ask you with a light gesture
to take a seat at the table, you,
who for uncertain reasons have sought me

and for a while have been leaning
over my table, rejected, shut out,
as though you didn't exist.

I pour water
in abundant quantities
in the grey misty light,

sweep like the wind through a willow
the shadow from your face,
turn a stream magnetically.

The world doesn't stop, though doors close,
mild, raw air you can inhale now,
draw breath easily again.

One moment settles
on top of another, without words,
like new snow covering the old.

I can't slow down time,
can't solve any riddles, but
I am here,

as long as you are here,
and you are here
as long as I am here,

movement, touch,
mutual exchange,
no complicated code,

that's how a veil is removed,
that's how we make the sky so big
that it smells of the first morning light.

Under cirrus clouds

Like blood springing out on a forehead,
bright red clouds of ice crystals
high above the earth, before the sun goes down,
compact smell of pine needles
is carried on a breeze from the trees further away.

A swarm of insects hangs in the air,
remember how it was to be kept awake
by a story without fighting sleep, just watch
lips in motion, listen to words from a mouth,
feel the warm breath flowing towards me,
keep me floating in the light of the lamp
like the insects in front of me.

Only after the story did I land in the dark,
which was good,
left to myself
words came bubbling out unceasingly.

I'm present, listen to my breathing in the middle of the path
where I've stopped,
as I heard my breathing in the dark as a child
without calling for anyone. My lungs

swelled out when the lamp was switched off,
the stories had no end in those days,
they kept on, incalculably,
there was no goodbye,
no one said that anything would end.

When one adventure finished, the next one went on,
there were only beginnings, becoming, openings,
as if the stories needed me

in order to unfold, or I needed them
in order to have life breathed into me, to draw breath,
so my lungs reached the sky, expanded
as now in the breeze under the cirrus clouds.

Your fragrance wakes me

The sea turns heavily in its sleep,
when you emerge
from the bath, my love.

When like the light you choose
the shortest distance towards me,
the fragrance moves ahead of you, warmth from your skin,
convincing me of
reason's inadequacy.

Your fragrance wakes
something invisible in me, deadens
the slightest doubt.

You arrive like the night that bursts
into the day, but here it is quiet,
not a sound is heard.

You touch me
with your fragrance, tenderly,
tickle me
with your fragrance, giddily,

your fragrance makes me
feel more naked,
I breathe in, more easily than before.

There is only one body,
and it is approaching now,
the space is filled by you,
it encloses me blindly.

Not yet the taste of your kiss,
not yet caresses, only
waves of our fragrances, they

meet, they mingle,
make the room expand
and draw back again.

You come to me like the night,
it will take as much as it wants,
from the day, erase the day. Soon.

Freezing fog

I see your breath swirl about you, see my breath hang
like a thinly spun cloud
when I speak,
see our breaths reach each other, dissolve,
fade away, as caresses will cease one day,
we know.

The cold sears when we breathe in,
the nose is pressed against winter coat's smell of wet wool,
when we put our arms around each other,
wish each other 'good day'
in the midst of our exertions with what must be fought with,
so that our lives don't collapse.

The chimneys are like plinths for smoke that rises
in the late autumn morning,
I see the smoke pulse above the city and the slippery roads.
Tiredness is written into the flesh, muscles quiver,
the blood circulates, there's a harsh jerking
in soul and nerve-ends, an inner avalanche,
when I go on, the road
has no forbearance if I turn around,
like a snorting animal I make my lonely imprint.

Lovesick bird

Draw breath in, as deep as I can,
shoulders rise and fall, light
rises and falls, the snow's aromatic light.

I'm three-dimensional,
if my lungs are unfolded they have an area
about the size of a 90 square metre
apartment, I move in,
put every corner to use.

Belly, back, my whole ribcage expands,
the dome-shaped diaphragm
that increases the volume of the cervix, swells up
when I draw breath, sucks in the fragrances around,
air, passage, movement,
I'm bright awake,
draw breath in, snowdrift, snowstorm, snow-winter,
at night snow-white moon-sabre.

I sing and speak on the air I breathe out,
sing standing while lifting my head
like a lovesick bird,
for does the bird sing with head bowed?

Draw breath in, as deep as I can,
like boarding a train north of the future
and let myself be carried off,
finding rest in movement, peace
to embrace an acoustic alphabet,
peace to form thoughts into words,
before I breathe out again beyond the white tracks of the snow lines.

II

Antitheses

Noses, a comparative study

From my seat on the plane I look up at noses
slowly filing past
in the narrow aisle, noses
from very different parts of the world
gathered this evening hour in a single place,

small and large, slim and wide, long and short,
curved and flat, snub noses, crooked noses,
sculptural noses, noses with a ring,
inconspicuous noses, arrogant noses,
pug noses and potato noses,
obviously corrected noses,
noses that carry spectacles on their bridge,
noses in highly varied colours, all

dig their way into the cabin's synthetic odour
or manage not to notice it
on their way to the right seat on a joint expedition
away from ice and frosty nights, each traveller
on the road to themselves.

Research methodically
the genetically diverse noses
intended for the same use,
noses each with a history of smell,
magical and massive,
a carousel of dizziness brings
any thought to a halt. The plane takes off,

ascends above the clouds in the lonely night,
where we sit for hours pupated
in mono-coloured blankets in a hovering
above the ocean, while the sky whirls around the plane.

With a smile the flight attendant serves
spring water with a fresh aroma of
sky and underground,
or is it sky and abyss?

Seduced by Gregory Pincus

Doped by years of the pill and as a result
with badly disturbed senses I allowed myself
half anaesthetised and with a slumbering soul
to be kissed by a man whose smell was different
than I noticed later, sour.

Where did it go wrong?
No warning traffic lights
for driving on sexual roads
flashed red in nights of
dream dust and shooting stars.

The fear of fear was totally erased
with Gregory Pincus' pills.
With my basic smell
I manoeuvred blind, had children,
who luckily for me smelled blessedly of mine.

Not a gift

The soap and deodorant on a colleague's desk
are not a gift from the many to the one
on a festive day,

those two objects are a signal to a living being,
a resounding tsunami warning,
the unambiguous logic of the place,
a hope for a new era, a space to breathe freely in,

though the chemical communication
of the recipient can't be seen as anything
but camouflaged results of cloned conspiracy,
uniformity's thunderous and endless scourge,
society's lifebelt thrown out to a swimmer.

What smells, smells,
the steaming vapour sets its hissing marks
on the hermetic room,
spreads like growth rings in the jungle's trees,
irritated nostrils quiver, smell a capsized future.

Tags in the night

A man turns his back on the world, sends his beam
up against the wall, frees his organism
of waste materials, here there's an intense smell of urine,
so on you go and leave your water here.
The warm urine spray of the first one calls on the second,
as dogs sniff for traces of other dogs,
put their smell markers in the territory,
stare up at the same selected lamp post.

The low rolling fog propagates widely
at the almost depopulated station after midnight.
The wall twists while the foul-smelling lake
flows over the asphalt, and the man quits the spot,
unlike cats, which with a paw
throw gravel or earth
over their leavings, cover
their tracks carefully each time.

The smell of ammonia visits me as I
get off the train. Already at a long distance
the stench cuts in like a dagger, the smell
of others' urine etches itself into the mucous
membranes of my nose, while the nature-called doesn't
smell himself, he does what suits him, relieves himself
and eases the pressure, refuses to submit,
numbingly indifferent to norms and considerations.

Here, urine doesn't serve as fertiliser for plants,
it doesn't recycle itself as a beneficial nutrient,
isn't used to tan leather,
is not included in pharmaceuticals or cosmetics.
Here in the public space the liquid isn't useful
in that way, it is simply left as a sign,

as a protest against an order devised by others,
left to annoy others, like tags sprayed

on the wall for a moment, a dimension of freedom.
I hold my breath for several seconds,
as I lurch past trying
not to get my shoes wet,
react like a compass with a crazy needle
until out in the open again my chest subsides.
I exhale slowly, gasp for air,
maybe poison the world with these lines.

Cleaning poisons

To make everything clean,
you remove algae from
the shower curtain with chlorine.

It's white again and just like new.

Dry faucets, rub pipes, keep
the limescale line in the bathtub away with
sponges dipped in acetic acid.

Everything glitters and is clear.

Use ammonia solution in the siphon trap
with hair and soap residues and
drain cleanings in the washbasin.

Everything works and is good.

Clean old paint residues
away with turpentine,
wipe mirrors with spirit.

Everything sparkles and is shiny.

Although the window is up and open
wide agape,
I breathe in fierce fumes.

Everything shines towards me.

My nose tickles
there's a clawing and scratching,
a pressing in my head, a throbbing.

Everything flickers in my eyes.

Grow dizzy,
sneeze again and again,
get my usual headache.

Everything flashes and glitters.

No one cleans as you do,
week after week,
year after year.

Everything shines, glows and is fine.

It's just me
who have my brain blown out, while you
loudly enjoy the chemistry and claim to be okay.

Them or us

Does the reality originate in an illusion
or is the illusion a reality:
a foreign smell in the familiar room,
I'm ten years old, people from another country
are visiting for the first time,
wearing colourful clothes around the table in the living room
on the farm away out in the countryside, green fields, sun.

Exotic presents, foreign eyes, ears, noses, mouths,
the smell penetrates the room, wanders without roots,
cuts through the conversation, drowns out
the meal, the exchanges
about differences between our language and theirs,
their culture and ours,
voices buried in the air, shadow words.

My father pours, the guests eat Danish food,
drink Danish beer, combine ingredients
on their plates that don't belong together,
while they talk about dishes from their part of the world,
the air seems poisoned, there's no lid for the smell,
it's there all the time, wonder if it's in their clothes,
or do they think we smell so horrible,
I huddle up, shiver with discomfort in the heat.

The earth whispers, we only hear it
a week later, the dead mouse
under the floorboards in the living room is revealed,
we touch the darkness, the shame, stand
with black eyes, staring,
the guests have long since gone home.

Digital odours

Smells can be sent digitally, says the announcer
on the radio. Will it someday broadcast more than sound,
will the radio emit a powerful reek of sulphur
when the discussion is of pig farms, a stench of glue
or burnt rubber from factories, automatically
bring smells of gas or hot blood
when reporting from war zones
from which millions of people are fleeing.

So far via an oPhone they have only
succeeded in sending the scents of champagne
and coffee and passion fruit
over the Internet from Paris to New York,
pictures, texts and videos are accompanied by aromas.

If radio, TV, mobile phone and other objects
acquire the ability to receive smells
we will slowly suffocate in our own homes.

If an olfactory language is installed, that one can voluntarily
choose to receive, with a little icon one can turn off
unwanted odours with streams of air,
block the physiological effect on one's own territory.

The wordless greetings may be tempting propositions
from restaurants and flower shops,
encouraging invitations between lovers,
developed in sophisticated smell laboratories,

but if you send a bouquet of the wine you
have opened, love,
I would rather come and sit down at your table
than make do with an olfactory impulse,
no matter how lovingly it's meant.

If planes, cinemas and shops install computer chips
that emit streams of smells,
I can't withdraw from the room, can't select
them. I will be sprayed away in clouds of fragrance.

The sense of smell is the one people can best imagine
living without, but smells drown out sounds, drown out sights,
a hateful smell sent by an enemy
is more than a powerful signal,
the tender nose runs, itches at the thought.

III

Meditation

Spring inhalation

The mirabelle trees turn the inside out to the light, rise
above the dust-brown soil like melted snow between the branches.

If the smell from the trees puts itself into a dream,
it will be able to call forth a smile in a sleeper.

The treetops open white and airy, clouds
stopped in their flight, caught by the trees' thorns.

A game with time, a lightness, a spring inhalation
of warm air under a hazy sky.

As waves bear salt foam and throw it high,
the trees stand in an explosion of flowers.

A ray of sunlight sweeps across the fields,
there is no reason not to draw one's breath.

I can narrow my attention, close my mouth
and eyes, but can't stop the smells, they penetrate.

Deep down in my chest, in the inverted crown of the bronchial tree,
I breathe the whiteness of the waves, the boundlessness.

From the trees a fragrance has moved into me,
that no one can take from me, not even I.

Exchange of smells

The smell of the newborn child flows warm
to greet me, a cloud of molecules emanates
from the tiny body,
my offspring.
A delicate and fluffy fragrance
that hasn't been in the world before,
shuts out everything else for a second.

The archaeological trowel
digs in the moment, my nose slides over
the child's cheek and forehead, its scalp,
time is.
Can't get enough of the new creature,
notice the room is filled with its fragrance.

An identical process starts in the child's brain,
the child knows the smell of its mother's body
as distinct from another woman,
the smell of the mother clings to it,
a first germ of truth to navigate by,
wordless.

The child presses its nose to my breast,
breathes in a world filled
with its mother's smell, united and separated,
the child gathers all the attention,
fear- and dream-cells grow
with unpredictable strength.

Danish cat meets Australian stone

Smells don't always vanish like shadows,
they can be ferried from one continent to another,
the smell of oranges, of dates and mango
seems refreshing in the North, just as
the cat now trance-like engrossed rubs its head
against a stone brought back from Australia to Denmark.

The cat is attracted by the unidentifiable smells
from a palm-sized grey stone full of holes
laid on the floor in the living room, it stretches neck and back,
rolls instinctively over the stone again and again,
rubs the foreign smells into it, deposits

its own smell on this particular exquisite stone,
as others plant their flag
on the summit of Mount Everest, on Svalbard, on Mars,
on the Moon, a flag of stainless titanium in the Arctic Ocean
under the North Pole, in the hope of making claims for oil and gas,
territorial markings, fleeting or for the future.

Smell of tomatoes

Raw and sweetly acidic smell tears at my nostrils
when I touch the leaves or yank
tomatoes from the stalk, one by one,
my tentacles pluck away at the clusters,
my hand grasps anything that's round.

Compressed fragrance in a hothouse filled
with man-size tomato plants surges up,
the heat, the moisture, the yellow star flowers
spring out
between the flying shadows of the leaves,
the ripe and unripe tomatoes,
green, red and all shades in between,
the tied-up plants with
bewildered, flirting side-shoots
stretching in an embrace with the light,
tomatoes in a struggle to grow the biggest,
the place is the smell.

Still always sharp, fresh, unmistakable
fragrance from the stalk, the hand's grip,
firm and careful, a rush
in the second the fruit
is yanked off,
stronger than the taste
of even the most sun-ripe tomato.

Smell-trace of a morning

Lie with eyes closed, don't yet know if I'll wake
to a world of love or hate,
the first thing I sense with all the sensors
in my nose and sinuses is the smell in the room,

the smell of skin, hair, nails, of wild creatures in the bedroom,
yesterday's black panthers unleashed,
though human shoes flow past the bed,
fragrance-heavy remnants of dreams glued to the brain,

fragrance of sleep-lifted hair, of sleep-rinsed,
hypersensitive morning skin, relaxed, pain-free
morning muscles, the daily resurrection
of the reflexes, fragrances of warm, naked sexes,

an acrid smell of morning urine in the toilet, intense mint-smell
of toothpaste when I squeeze it out of the tube, fragrance
of the warm, lime-rich water from the shower, of wet skin,
of wet hair, olive-scented shower gel, fruity shampoo,

vegetable aroma of cream deodorant, faint smell
of beeswax in the day cream for the face, in the winter skin lotion,
odourless ointment for wounds, lesions and torments of the soul,

sweaty, sticky, dirty smells from yesterday
cling to my clothes, I replace them with smells
of newly washed clothes fetched out of the closet.

The fragrance fills out from the steam-filled bathroom,
the kitchen emits smells of food from yesterday, smoke
from an adjacent room finds its way through cracks,
drowns out the subtly spicy spring smell

of winter aconite placed in a cream jug on the table,
the smell orgy from the dish of fruit and vegetables,
faint floral smell of fine-leaved Assam tea
from districts by the River Brahmaputra in north-west India,

the grain cracker smelling of rye flour, the nutty
smell of a firm cheese or white mould smell of a brie,
the peapod-smelling peppers, the vitamin pill's chemical smell,

sharply sour smell-drops from citrus peel split the second,
call forth a tremor of unease around the cat's whiskers,
the sum of everyday smells that are again drowned by the air

from an open window because each morning the clean
changes places with the dirty, as when
the filled rubbish bag is taken down and a fresh one is set up,
new smells sweep through the room now,

smells of drizzle, wet tree-trunks, wet asphalt, bird-calls,
smell of the incomprehensible, the material, cinders, something on the way,
the smell from the mug filled with steaming hot Mexican coffee

with freshly boiled milk, triggering each morning a violent sneeze,
the sweet fragrance of coffee at once makes itself stand out
as the only thing I perceive, penetrates,
tickles its way into the nose's walls to prepare for the day's work.

Camellia japonica

Listen to a friend's English words
laden with Japanese accent,
while I smell
newly loomed camellias in the park
in the middle of Tokyo near the Imperial Palace,
deep inside, where the paths are pierced
by gnarled tree roots, and I
am filled by the day.

The voice belongs to his face,
his words become song, as we walk
between rocks and earth
near the water that flows further down.
Lines in his brain lead
like longitudinal axes in an atlas
to a shared, almost intact
story I've heard fragments of before,
until his words are interrupted
by crows in the air above the trees.

Suddenly, the absence of speech becomes
hermetic silence, when we stop
on our way up the steep slope
by the water, where nothing other
than our breath can be deciphered,
and a cataract of smells around us
strikes deep roots that no one can run from.

Benchmarks from a long day

Smell makes nostrils vibrate,
the smell of the morning's sunny warmth in the room,
of faces that love me,
of the sun in the grass, the sun in the dog's coat,
of lofts with bats, of toads in damp cellars,
of wardrobes, of my mother's sleepless nights,
of topsoil, of well water, rubber boots,
of the bog, the brook, of a grass-snake through the meadow,
of mud and mire, of anemones on the floor of the woods,
of clover, rapeseed, of poppy fields,
of strawberry plants, stalks of rhubarb, of blue grapes,
of mouldy berries, rotten apples, rotten pears under the trees,
of the horse's mane, its muzzle, of a foal in the grass,
of the grain in the barn, of the dust in the beam of light, the animals
    in the stalls,
of silage, clamps, feed, milk,
of excrement and dead piglets on the dunghill,
of henhouse, of foxes' earth, slaughtered animals,
of entrails, animals in carved pieces,
of sowing seed in flaxen sacks, of haystacks in the field,
of burned stubble fields, harrowed earth,
of spruce, orange, of nuts, cinnamon and cloves,
of snowy air, of snowy fields, slush,
of packed lunches kept in the schoolbag,
of warmed-up liver paste, meat sausage, egg sandwich,
of pencil cases, classrooms, bubble gum,
of book bus and school libraries,
of workshops, oil, of scrap bins and spare parts,
of saltwater, fish and tar, of harbour jetties, dried seaweed,
of botanical flowerbeds, of a whole zoo,

the smell of fresh blood, of clotted blood,
of skin, of a body like a sea of light, a white coast,

of tenderness, of caresses, gushing desire,
of towns, of streets, bars, rendezvous,
of cafes, of bookstores, squares and marketplaces,
of letters, of wine in the glass, future and euphoria,
of the road onwards, of the immense horizon,
of fledglings in the nest, of morning mist,
of fields, woods, lakes in the woods,
of full-blooded full moon nights and propagation,
of a love child, of umbilical cord, of placenta,
of songs, bedtime stories, card games,
of reading hours with a child on one's knee,
of bare feet in the grass, of kites above the trees,
of bonfires, of caves, catching of jellyfish in fishing nets,
of freshly baked bread, of mirrors without masks,

the smell of the sky strikes roots, the smell of little avalanches,
of changes, invisible transformations,
of sweat, of worn soles, tired muscles, tired souls,
of nerves of stone, of anger and excitement, pitfalls,
of exhaustion from coping with the day, interruptions,
of exertion to overcome resistance,
of hearts in battle, of shattered dreams,
of beginningless beginnings,
of doubts, of cessations, collapsed ideas,
of the darkness of despair, of crisis nights, shards,
of packed suitcases, of strangers' fingerprints in the passport,
of journeys between the possible and impossible,
of places of refuge, empty spaces, of longing to travel and homesickness,
of faces I love
of wild orchids that fill the air with their scent,
of open wounds, of blood-spattered war-shadows,
of the earth, of the crown of the tree over the bench by the water,
of the roots of the alphabet, of dreamed poems,
of ink, of rain falling, snow falling,
of breathless blood, of the heart's skewed beats in the words,
of meditative evening thoughts, of the wisdom of the wind,

of its changing directions,
the smell makes nostril vibrate,
the accumulating brain record time and memory.

IV

Bloodstreams

Wrong number

Snow in April, sleet and hail, it gets dark at noon.
On the phone a woman I don't know,
she needs a nurse, calls cold
without saying her name, drops flicker,
glints of ice in the air.

Here there is no nurse, no gauze, nothing
that can stanch a bleeding wound,
there is a smell of wet air, of silence, elevation,
a few balls of hail fall amidst the delicate green,
while I talk to the woman, smells

from the street smack in through the open window,
smells of spring, of cold and showers,
a sudden storm of hail cuts, disfigures.
I listen to the woman who lost
herself, she asks if it is always night-time,
hail-white wings spread out, sharply,
rustle, flap at shifting intervals.

For eternities I listen,
the woman no longer needs a nurse.

Sleepwalker-like
I return to my papers, to the circumference
of my aloneness, to the poem I was writing,
note with restless heart that I
don't recognise it now, not even as a dream.

Under the asphalt the Milky Way

In the park the leaves tumble down,
lie on the wet soil,
emit an odour
of urge towards darkness,
free fall.

Your overfilled glass
and after that another
and yet another, so many
that bottles fall over, houses
collapse.

The night's footsteps supported
by the row of cars
along the kerbs,
the light from the street lamps
skates over the asphalt.

The film about the city is
suddenly played backwards,
your head sinks down,
falls.

A burning meteor
smashes against asphalt and earth,
against a silence
I only know from
reading rooms here

or museums in Japan,
where custodians exchange
scratching ballpoint pens
for soundless pencils
to make notes about a bloody world.

Garlic

The spring had arrived,
and the boys, magnetic
assignations in Hellebæk woods
or by the water on Langebro Bridge.

The spring had arrived,
with a hard hand
my mother controlled
the meetings with the boys,

dosed her dishes
not by chance with garlic,
that was always
within reach,

dosed my bloodstream,
my over-wintered cells,
according to who rang
breathless to make a tryst with me.

The spring had arrived,
the evenings were lighter,
abducted birds sang, I
sang and stank of garlic,

each evening worse
than the last, for
my mother didn't care
for the local boys there.

The spring had arrived,
and the boys, I breathed in,
breathed out, but in the dream
the dream was only dreamt.

Nose to the ground

Are there narcotics and intoxicating substances
in the luggage from Copenhagen to Malmö.

Is something illegal being transported
across the Sound in bags and suitcases.

By the sense of smell a salmon trout moves
thousands of kilometres through rivers and streams.

Customs officials go through the train with a dog,
whose muzzle sniffs up the air carriage by carriage.

With its antennae
a male moth can register

just a single smell molecule from a female
at up to a distance of around five kilometres.

The dog sniffs for narcotics and chemicals,
is able to smell concentrations

hundreds of thousands of times smaller than I can,
it stops in front of a bag in the compartment,

has its raised muzzle smelled trouble.
All at once the dog detects something, scrapes its paw,

the passenger opposite sits perfectly still, I
sit perfectly still, listen to his breathless blood.

A forgotten smell suddenly, the smell of myself.

The cream from China

On the plane back from Shanghai
an Asian man on the seat
next to me asks for permission
to smell my hands,
but they belong to me and not to him,
doesn't he understand that.

I have smeared my hands with a cream
from a small yellow metal tin with flowers
on a blue background
with gold and red characters
I cannot read,

ah I want to kiss the hand
put my mouth on it and eat the whole thing,
writes Sakutarō Hagiwara.

I have smeared my hands with a cream
whose smell he recognises from afar,
my hands smell

of snow white lilies, he says,
and apparently with tears and silent sorrow
he misses his wife,

but he will have to go on doing that,
he is violating my sphere, has no right
to approach my fragrance,
though I obviously share it
with his wife, as well as
the blood's murmur under the skin. I'm the angel

with the fiery sword, watch
over my hands,
draw them towards me,
a man I don't know
shall not lift them to his face,
press his lips to them,

ah I would like to gratefully receive one smoothly
    polished finger
have it slip into my mouth and suck on it, suck on
    it forever and ever,
writes Sakutarō Hagiwara.

V

The five seasons.
A catalogue of smells

Spring

Smell of melted ice and light that dazzles white,
of sea-cold wind that streams over land, of sun
that fills the vapour-heavy air, smell of wet fields,

smell of snowdrops, of winter aconite, crocus, coltsfoot and violet
locally anaesthetises the air here, as the bush full of sparrows
initiates the day with an undecipherable song,

smell of dust from pollen, of half a ton of freshly-turned
earth in the form of shots from mole, subterranean,
yet also perceptible firework display for the nose,

smell of cold, that now sticks close to the earth,
the mist creeps forward in waves in the first light of dawn,
as when something not expected approaches and overpowers,

smell of tender green leaves and at the same time my mother's
melancholy, as her nails scratch dirt from the glass pane, smell
of stains, soot and cobwebs, that unambiguously emerge,

smell of sun, that in turn flows from a gap in the cloud, smell
of long shadows thrown out into the light, inscrutable
moments wash in and drive home like a mighty swell,

smell of burnt bridges, of shipwrecks and new abysses
to go plunging down, as we dive quietly into each other
so as not to drown completely in an inane indifference,

smell of powerlessness, smell of the horror of being weakened
in the midst of what sprouts and pulses,
smell of nightmares and night time fear of final ending,

smell of wet stains, plaster that decays, crumbles
like old skin peeling off in long flakes,
smell of soap, smell of lye and mortar, slaked lime,

smell of coffee in cafés filled with guests wrapped in blankets,
while a boy in the sun goes from table to table, begging,
the smell of waking up in the light, returning strong,

smell of spring, of a handful of joy and another
full of inexplicable sorrow, that constitutes the day
with the bright light, at the same time an open grave.

Summer

Smell of sea, of onshore wind by coastal slope, of sand
and beach and sun-warm skin, of salt in hair, smell of the body's
summer-sensitive nerves, smell of meadow and mushrooms, jasmine
and wild roses, smell of honeysuckle, smell of elder, of cherries
in the tree, plundered by a huge flock of starlings, of broken birds' eggs,

smell of swathe-cut clover, smell of laburnum, wisteria, roses' hot
rose skin, of butterfly dust, of blossom snow falling red
in the evening light, smell of dregs in glasses on garden table, smell of party
dresses dissolved in a lukewarm shower, of sweetish blood, when the tick
searches for food with eight legs that tickle across the ankle,

smell of great beech trees' coolness, of the shade beneath them,
of the moss between oak and pine and birch, of sun in resin, smell
of carrion devoured by ants in busy progress on the forest floor,
as we draw away from the path system between trunks
and a network of unruly, rotten branches, find our way into silence,

smell of past, myriad smell-trails into narrow alleys, smell
of the smoke from my grandfather's Old Havana, as he drove on
the warm asphalt road, while I as a child travel sick behind
his seat had to vomit in torrents, smell
of rich petrol and autocratic driving round every bend in the city,

smell of my other grandfather's whiskey breath, smell of masculine and fresh
shaving lotion when I sat there drunk with fragrance on his knee,
my older cousin on the other, while we were told stories, especially
about our fathers, when they were reckless, naughty boys,
anecdotes that could easily erase melancholy thoughts,

smell of dust, in a thousand manifestations, of the homeless in the city
streets, smell of sour air mattresses on a ventilator grill, a bag
stuffed with dirty clothes, string shopping bag with cans of beer, of
us gazing down at the pavement slab and a handful of coins for
the empty cup in the attempt to walk past and not feel shame,

smell of organic life, of brutal crimes committed
in my own country with the stench of murder, of bestial assaults
at night time, of rape, blood, incest, wrongdoing
carried out in secret against the near or distant, smell of the body's
terrified cells like the acrid smell of foxes' earths,

smell of rain steaming gently and striking roofs, roads, cars,
paving stones, trees, grass-blades, smell of the water that vainly tries
to lift us, to wash the world clean again, to purify it of sludge
and clotted algae, of guilt, deceit and falsehood, of lies, concealment
and callousness, of incurable wounds that we must live with.

Autumn

Smell of autumn, of cold clouds across the sky, smell
of wild geese pulling away in wedges from the Nordic zone,
smell of leaves fluttering to the ground, smell of nuts,
smell of apples' thud from tops of trees,

smell of seed and grain in barn, smell of dust, of grain for feed,
seed, bread and malt, of oats, wheat, barley,
of rye, of grass and oilseed rape, when air
in drying units is blown through tall heaps,

smell of the plough's turned furrows, smell of wind in hair, the boy's
warm scalp as he storms around in the wood
and field with the other boys until the sweat is leaping,
and the twilight darkness creeping out from every side,

smell of rowan berries, of late roses, smell of snowberries, golden leaf-fall,
of chestnut trees' shiny brown fruits, smell of onion
and marrow, cabbage and carrot, of new potato harvest,
the last sun-dried tomatoes before the frost sets in,

smell of heavy grape-clusters, smell of elderberry and blackberry,
smell of ripe pears, figs, plums, peaches, smell
of hurled honey, sudden embrace in the October sun's
warm rays, smell of the night sky with shooting stars,

smell of mushrooms deep in woodland moss, of seasoned air, of splendid
russula, leccinum and suillus, smell of poisonous fly agaric,
of chanterelle and porcini visited by snails and by us hunting
with knives and baskets, armed with an endless patience,

smell of crumpled leaves, of dry straw and withered grass,
of chopped timber from a fallen tree, of wood when axe blows
make the wedge split the log, smell of pine cones, twigs
and firewood ready for frost and long winter days,

smell of rain and rough weather, of leaves of trees, that now cling wet
like old men to their wives, smell of the grass's sour blades,
of sodden haystacks, of compost, of rain-soaked cattle
on the field, smells after heavy rain, smell of newfound calm,

smell of slaughtered cattle, of blood and fear of loneliness
and eternal unease, stench of killings in another part of the world,
smell of anxiety and distant wars, brutality of the universe
breathed in with moist air and far from hopeful labour pains.

Winter

Smell of minus degrees, mornings without light, and short days,
smell of sombre clouds, smell that heralds more snow on the way,
of icicle-rows under roofs, smell of hibernating creatures, of children
sleeping one eye open while ice blooms freely on the pane,

smell of winter cold, snow that swirls, snow on cars, that
are filled with coolant, duvets of snow on the roofs, snow on bushes,
snow that lines birds' nests, smell of frozen sprouts and leeks,
smell of ice-covered raspberries among dry herbs,

smell of winter woods, where squirrels seek their hidden nuts and acorns,
smell of snow on pine and fir trees, smell of moss and cones, smell
of snow on roads and paths, smell of frozen puddles, smell
of heavy boots crunching through ice and down into stone and mud,

smell of winter fields, smell of frozen grass blades under snow
on the meadow, smell of horses at the filled-up feeding place
where the steam is like dragons' breath from their muzzles, smell
of horse with winter coat, of horse manure, where crows are pecking,

smell of snow in sun, of diamonds' play in the light, smell of winter life,
when hares jump around in the snow, slight traces of animals
one frost-filled day, a smell in the house under the kitchen sink,
where a mouse is bashfully looking for food in a garbage can,

smell of cleared snow in great heaps, smell of frozen lakes where
we stand on skates, children and adults, so that the metal cuts down
into the ice, and the warm breath billows through the air when we talk
about the frozen spider's web that swings in the low sun,

smell of winter, smell of clarity, smell of purity mixed up
with chimney smoke, while the snow illuminates the winter night,
so the darkened landscape lights up in the moonlight, a radiance
on endless, peaceful surfaces no map can cover,

smell of bitter cold starry sky above nocturnal snow that the dog
shakes out of his coat, snow that erases all limits,
silent gleams and aurora borealis dreams from polar zones
that with cold winds' sighing bewildered find their way to me,

smell of winter, smell of wildernesses, ice crystals flame white,
where the snow falls thick and silent, until it melts again,
knocks me over in great drifts, washes the back of my neck with
those cold clumps that only slowly melt down my spine.

The fifth season

The smell of the fifth season drowns out things that have
enchanted: Snowdrops and winter aconite have disappeared,
likewise tulip and narcissus, also cornflower
and lupins are a thing of the past like asters,

the smell of the fifth season hangs like a wild
cloud of memory, vibrates amid the light, settles
in nostrils and lungs, soul, it takes its origin in all
the seasons, continues swirling on in a sublime spiral,

the smell of the fifth season contains the weather's
unbroken changes, sun, that alternates abruptly with the rain,
that's followed hard by hail, and then a gale,
raging between houses, finding its way into narrow crevices,

the smell of the fifth season is a shower
on leaves of trees, trees that flames are nourished with,
and fire, that again shapes the earth the metal
is retrieved from, metal that in turn is water catalyst,

the smell of the fifth season is not fully sensed,
only perceived, the fifth season always consists of now
and not next year and next, the smell of the fifth season
is a labyrinthine demand, requires a quantum leap,

the smell of the fifth season transfigures, above all,
so it is flesh that turns into earth, and earth
that's reshaped when the sky acquires its colour-play
of dust, and the dust, by inversion, the shades of heaven,

the smell of the fifth season shows life broken up by
anxiety's lightning, composition replaces decomposition,
the new arises with beauty's smell particles entrapped
by the mind's fear of chaos-storms and powerlessness,

the smell of the fifth season awakens the brain's sidereal years,
utopian smell as of a fine membrane, a hitherto
invisible opening, from which I can escape
with unknown pulse, disappear in words of transformation.

VI

Flashes of thought

Caught in the act

The fish catches its food
and itself is caught, has its head
cut off with a cracking sound,
the smell of fish blood rises while
under the knife the fish still twitches.

The light bones and feathers
lie scattered among grass and stones,
where the bird circled in the air,
smelled its way to earthworms in the soil,
before the marten consumed its meal.

On the grassy plains a hungry wolf
goes after the sheep's bellies and guts,
on the carcasses the ribs
are gnawed away, flies and worms
take care of the last remnants.

In the dust among the rubble of war
the wounded lie,
I recognise the smell,
when an angel breaks.

In the dust among the rubble of war
lie the dead,
victims of a bloody hour, who once
lay in wombs,
must now be placed in the grave
infinitely close to our hearts.

Breathing, collision,
the locations accumulate,
rocks and clods of earth,
the whole world is a crime scene.

Smell blind

It's strange,
but I don't remember your smell
when you're not here, you said.

That reply made me put
the perfume away for a long time.
That you couldn't distinguish
one woman's fragrance from another
hadn't dawned on me yet.

My nose to your throat
and chest, I sniffed
your scent as a dog
ploughs its muzzle through the autumn leaves,

my soul is full
of smells,
I loved your scent, it hung

not only in the air where you had been,
it existed like an echo
in my memory,
as if lightning had struck there.

Without the perfume my skin smells
again of me, and the poems
I write may very well smell of skin,
for of all conceivable lives I prefer this one.

The meaning of meaninglessness

The room darkens, like a cupola
closes around us, faces are extinguished.

Snow rolls forward, recognised
as nothingness, void,
meaninglessness I not infrequently
take root in, roads without goals,
roads that change as soon as
one starts walking, places
abandoned forever.

The sky opens in a roar,
far away and close to, lets the smells in
through the open window.

The lungs' petals
breathe the boundless in,
a wave propagates out
to the outermost parts of the body,

deeper I don't fall, the blood
flees in the veins' channels, is overtaken
by a burning pain
that with surgical precision
finds a point in the heart,
bores its way in with barbs.

We die,
side by side when we have coupled,
for a moment drunk on our breathing,
soul divided from soul, each with our smell

ceaselessly sniffed in
from the snow-filled space above us,
as if someone were longingly present.

After showers of bullets in paradise

Each day is a decision to live
the life I was born to live,
I draw breath when I'm asleep, when I'm awake,
when I love, when I struggle
with the dread that unexpectedly rolls like thunder,

and these days I am angry,
because dread again
has sought me out just
when I thought I had a hiding place,
but the aggression isn't new,
even in finds

from Stone, Bronze and Iron Age
there are signs of brutal murders
and conflicts, violence
has existed at all times,
broken skulls, skeletons with traces
of assault, murdered dreams, violence

arises under pressure, accelerates under pressure,
battle-axes in Iron Age graves speak
a hellish language,
it wasn't only hunting tools
the dead could take with them on the journey,
fanaticism and hatred live

in the same world as I,
right next to me, draw breath
when I'm asleep, when I'm awake,
take the air from my lungs in little jerks
when the dread leaps out, settles
in my clothes like a strange odour.

I must again try to breathe easily
on a continent where blood flows
after showers of bullets and mental wounds
have settled in the soul, draw breath
in the freely moving chaos, where hatred
sometimes pretends to be an embrace.

Words without smell

At night fluids wash through the brain
to sleep's calm breathing,

a real chemical dry cleaning,
I wake up, the smells

are penetrating
in the sunrise, the earth smells,

I have been woken by my own body's
creaking, by the blood's movement.

The smell of grass
is strong and fresh,

the grass's molecules settle
on pearls of water, the dewdrops

that grow denser in the evening
evaporate in the morning,

when atoms break the bond
to neighbouring atoms in the drops.

The fox's euphoria in the damp grass,
when it sticks up its muzzle to sniff the scents,

stays standing still in the cool air,
for a long time on the same spot. It is quiet here,

but somewhere else on the globe survivors search
after an earthquake with masks on nose and mouth

for dead, to bury them by the river,
father is buried, mother is buried, brother.

VII

Vanishing

The smell can be parted from the body

Someone is always going away,
I run into a friend on his night-long wandering,
he embraces me in the street after all this time,
nomadic, turns on his heel, frost-prints.

Someone is always going away,
my neighbour rings my doorbell, surprises with her latest exploits,
the door is closed again, in my hands the cinnamon-scented cake,
footsteps out on the staircase fade away.

Someone is always going away,
a person, I fall into conversation with on the bus, have to get off
at the next stop, through the window I see him flit away,
no name, see him vanish in the crowd.

Someone is always going away,
the two young people I meet by the shelves in a bookshop,
show me the stack of books they've just bought, they wave,
rise suddenly like birds and are gone.

Someone is always going away,
my beloved arrives, he lands, unpacks,
kisses me hello and goodbye,
travels back to his own country, my soul stands naked in mine.

The horizon is scanned, convex, they have all been here,
The nose's compass needle detects it,
only waves of smell hang after them like echoes in the air.

Reflection on snow and ice

The smell of snow is good, the snow tells no lies,
it's there when it's there, like a snowstorm
or a chorus of snowflakes in the air, is not
like the sign on the shop door:
Back soon.
The snow settles as a greeting from a distant sky,
so far away my nose sniffs it in, my blood
is lit up by the snow, one thought grasps the next,
without a knot being tied.

Walk upright through the snow in icy cold,
my boots gnaw at my heels,
the sun makes the crystals shine, a blue-purple shadow
stands out in the white, which even in the darkness
tries to light the landscape.
My boots sink into the snow with each step,
as if solid ground were missing.

Think of polar bears hunting for food,
of reports that male polar bears have started
to mate with brown female bears,
because they sense instinctively
that the ice is melting, and only females
can teach their young to survive.

The winter has written off the snow,
it's not just the delete key
that has removed it with a single click,
it fell on but a few days this year, covered
the earth and the heart only just.

It was simply my brain that formed it
from a single syllable, I, who dreamt it,
dreamt that I walked in snow and frost,
in the boundlessness, weak and happy,
afraid that the snow had left the world
after reading about melted ice at sea,
about how polar bears, stranded on land,
must survive on body fat
from the spring hunting, and now make do
with birds' eggs and berries.

Think of polar bears hunting seals and fish,
think of snow as drops,
ice as drops,
the ice at the poles melts slowly, I learn
to draw breath in scorching heat, water flows.

Intense lethargy

I fly into myself
to be somewhere,

the night grows denser
in the blood,

the moonlight eliminates
the possibility of sleep,

one of my hands holds
the other by the hand,

one of my hands
touches the other,

the hand that touches
does not feel touched,

loneliness is not
for someone else,

it's only *my* breast
it bursts

in a space
that can barely breathe,

mild night,
time files itself away,

the smell of rain falls,
still without sleep coming.

Glenmorangie Highland Single Malt

The whisky I have preferred, since my future
began to shrink, comes flickering to meet me
with its gently spiced, honey-like scent,
Glenmorangie Highland Single Malt Scotch Whisky,
The Lasanta, extra matured in sherry butts,
like oranges and sweetly stored raisins,
walnut and caramel.

I don't miss a fireplace with a fire, the whisky
gives a sting of inner warmth,
when I swallow the golden drops
my tongue is wetted, comes alive,

then the liquid slides like a glacier
past the day's sharp edges, flows like fire
down the mountain slope, from oral cavity, throat,
through the oesophagus to the stomach,
the valley or the sea, where the glacier calves,
flames rise up.

I have seated myself in the day's last sunlight
let my gaze vanish away above the city's roofs,
while others bustle on the floors above me and below.
I have taken the best seat in the house,
regard the whisky-coloured sky in the west,
a glacier is only a glacier if it's moving.

Find myself smiling when you look at me,
also settle down to take a glass, and I,
gradually as the whisky sinks in the bottle,
and light blends with light
like long, soft aftertaste of a truth serum,
suddenly with the strength of a Gulf Stream
recall a life's pulsation, fleeting traces
it may soon be too late to find in the ruins.

The end of icebergs

I breathe in, in the dry air, fill
my lungs with a universe, breathe
an inner space out again.
The smell of icebergs, broken from glaciers in deep fjords
under the raw sky, hangs in the nostrils,
frost flies under the sun.

An iceberg sticks up through the sea's surface,
the young icebergs a couple of thousand years old, the older ones
with hundreds of thousands of years behind them.
Snowflake on snowflake, each
with its unique structure, have become
compressed, sleepless snow,
become mountains of ice, formations
widely different from other formations.

An iceberg gasps and gapes, forms
slits and cracks, breaks as if struck
by an invisible wedge, a giant colossus falls.
My chest opens out, I breathe in,
breathe out again, my breathing's space
connects with the world, forms a bridge,
I spread along airways out into space.

The mountains of ice collapse, the words
'snow' and 'ice' don't exist in Hebrew,
here one must find other words when the snow falls,
but what alternatives refer to
sleet, drifting snow, snowdrifts and other phenomena.
I straighten my back, smell the world, gather
a multitude of smells at once.

The mountains of ice collapse on hot days,
white ice-colours, grey, turquoise blue, crumbled blocks
rock and toss, turns their bottoms up
like creatures in a struggle for survival, roll
around and around in the water, run with the flow,
melt down to uniform drops in the open sea,
that rises transoceanic, wipes all trace of the ice's history.

VIII

Inner world, outer world

The smell greets me

I return home. My own smell
leaps to meet me when I step inside,
I suddenly think about the smell,
which I don't when I'm at home.

I notice myself as I sniff in
the smell with other people's noses,
perceive how they experience
my smell when they breathe in.

If they feel pleasure or discomfort, I don't know,
just that they detect an odour that isn't theirs,
the smell familiar to me is for them
the smell of another, a stranger.

My nose has smelled many people,
the smells of by far the most are quickly gone again,
there are very few I don't forget, but my own
I recognise sleepwalker-like each single time.

I return to my smell. Or it comes
to me, a smell-trail I have dragged from room to room
in the apartment, every time it's the smell that greets me
first, bids me welcome like a hungry carnivore.

Memory bank for smells

The moisture in the nasal cavity dissolves fine smell particles
to flowing form,
so around 40 million olfactory neurones
can capture a countless number of smells
to send them to the olfactory bulb,
the connecting link between nose and brain,
that transmits smell information,

so I can easily distinguish the smell
of my love's sweater from somebody else's,
the different herbs with worn-out labels;
rosemary, marjoram, thyme and basil,
so I can survive
by knowing the difference between spoilt food and fresh,

so I can smell my way to edible berries in the woods
among all the other smells, fragrances of berries,
that make me remember my grandmother's wild strawberries
in the shade under the quince tree, my mother's baskets
of blackberries from the field boundary, my sister's
earliest jam-making experiments with wild raspberries,

make me remember that the smell of a Skovfoged apple
is joy, an earthen smell identical to an abandoned house,
the smell of blood flowing over the floor connects
with sadness, sudden sweat, leaping out,
with my own fear, while the smell of warm milk is comfort.

Insect wing

The morning balances on a scent trail
of perfume planted in the air.

An insect wing beats between the houses,
spreads the scent of the drop,

dips the air, fills the city's space
on a busy and early morning, the scent

rises stageless in strength, navigates
with the blood's expectancy

against noses, binds
without straps, chains, ropes,

rubs the nostrils,
makes thoughts collapse,

splinters the morning, scent-seconds walk
on the wild side far into the day.

Nausea – a flashback

Even the smell of fennel when you're pregnant
is enough to make you throw up
across the stone floor of the Italian monastery,
where only visitors in good health
are welcome,
the sick and ailing must stay at home.

I arrive through hairpin bends
on narrow roads at the monastery on the mountain,
am greeted first thing
by the smell of steamed heads of fennel
and am feeling queasy
before the meal is served.

The smell penetrates from the kitchen in the basement
up to my cell, invades me,
it's impossible to keep to the monastery's rules,
on the first evening I have already broken them
with a heavy sea of vomiting.

The nausea is not existential,
one day fennel with a taste of liquorice and anise,
the next a dish of melted cheese,
smells from the outer world climb stairs,
walk through doorways and corridors, find their way
to my writing desk,
I can't yet make it safely down to the dining room.

I have come to the monastery to get peace,
have devoted my life's first grant to a month here,
but don't write a single poem this November,
I've moved in, I lie on the bed
with a child in my belly,
most of the time with sweat on my brow.

Smells filter daily into my room,
I am in an early pregnancy I didn't know about
when I applied for the visit,
I have violent nausea, throw up
at the very thought of the smell of the food,
while, certainly with great love, it's prepared.

Stink

There are people who can't endure their own smell,
the one that is theirs but to which they can't possibly put words.

People who bathe and scrub themselves,
but nevertheless feel disgust at themselves.

People who try to hide their own smell
under cover of creams and perfumes.

People who carry around wet tissues
to be able to clean themselves in acute situations.

People who constantly change diet
in an attempt to alter their body odour.

Drop coffee, cigarettes, garlic, cut down
on proteins that make a sulphur smell.

People who take magnesium, zinc
or other supplements in the hope of changing their smell.

People who take pills because they're afraid
their insides have started to decay.

People who test their hormone balance
in the hope of regulating their way out of the problem.

People who visit one doctor after another
to get rid of their own smell.

People who test their homes, smell if it's damp,
smell if it's mouldy or musty, is that where the smell comes from.

People who wonder if their body is worn out by stress
or pollution, if the problem comes from within or without.

There are people who turn their backs on others,
in order not to expose them to unpleasant smells.

People who think they smell disgusting,
even when those around them don't feel the least discomfort.

People who sense their own smell
as if they were reacting to a poisonous creature.

People who are in hell in their own body,
night falls, shuts everyone out.

Flower shop

My steps lead me to the flower shop,
down the stairs, into bouquets
on shelves and floor in the narrow room, I
stop at the sight of the colours in the winter cold,

am immediately struck by the fragrances, an acute attack
of discomfort in the store where the flowers emit
light, balsamic scents, heavy scents,
seasoned, perfumed, each species has its scent.

In bucketfuls the colourful bouquets spread out,
flowers in bud like a flicker of sequins,
flowers in the process of closing up, wide open
flowers gape and turn their insides out.

Side by side, flowers for party and funeral,
scents of longing, arousing scents,
scents of melancholy, numbing and nauseating scents,
they don't fall silent but grow in intensity.

My feet are nailed in front of the sea of flowers,
where the fragrances spread out in a shower,
I heave a deep sigh, am unable to accommodate
the sum of all the scents, grow dizzy and can't grasp

the moment, when I reflect myself in the cloud of scents,
when the mind's windows are broken, and ice-flowers are scattered
in shards, blood-flowers drip blood out over the floor,
and the brain's snow colours suddenly fill the room.

The primordial brain

Unmistakable smell of fire,
the instinct intact, even immersed in sleep,
the smell a hard flick
like a whiplash,
shakes the heart, keeps the soul prisoner.

Even a burnt slice of bread in the toaster,
sounds a black alarm,
the primordial brain reacts intuitively,

recognises in a split second the stinging smell of smoke
as smoke,
smell of something burnt, smell of soot.

An evolution of more than a hundred million years
since the fire
gives us a nose for just that smell,
burnt out, burnt down, charred,
piercing black presence, always.

IX

One breath makes the difference

Attack in Copenhagen

With a series of shots
a mirror image of the day is given,

draw breath in, breathe out,
death's door
opens quite easily.

A lonely young man in a bulletproof vest
is armed with several
high calibre weapons,

at home it's not our home,
when someone is killed,
the memory of tomorrow
is suddenly not there.

The vaccine isn't optional,
we get our injection of reality
installed in all the body's cells.

The police track the young man, he opens fire
on the officers, who respond with shots,
he collapses,
as if he were diving without weight

for something inside him, then he lies flat
on his back on the pavement, lifeless
one early grey and chilly morning with smell
of bloodstained February.

We gaze at each other, exchange looks,
try to regain a calm breathing,
regain confidence, the world is still open,
one breath makes the difference.

Welcome, people live here

Smells cannot be added, they mingle free
and unrestricted, submit to new laws,
go on imperceptibly living, people live here,
here you can sometimes hardly catch your breath,
here it stinks of week-old sweat, of cat piss,

of mould, rotten eggs, bad breath,
sweaty feet, turds, of vomit, sewer smell,
of internal organs in decay, like a stench
of rotten fish, clotted blood, infections,
of the germs in the air, drug deposits.

Can one learn to like these smells, or
merely put up with them out of necessity,
the air is not only clean and fresh, although
the breath grows ready to fly towards the sky,
it's just the wind that loves me today.

I want to be a tree

I have lost my way for a long time,
in fog, in sun, in nocturnal darkness,
in ice-hard blast, in pouring rain,

have gasped phobically for air,
wandered around like alphabet letters
that haven't yet found their poem,

now I want to be a tree in the park for a while,
share the globe with other trees, rest
in myself, breathe in,

that deep breath
from earth to heaven,
stretch my roots, straighten my trunk,
spread out my leaves, feel light in my heart,

observe an almost explosive
state of peace, when the wind
penetrated by the grammar of fragrance

writes on my leaves, sets them in motion,
so they light up, and birds
can fly through my crown, singing, screaming.

Twelve breaths

Sudden smell of hail
from the sky down over the city's roofs,
the ice-balls chase through the air.

Twelve breaths a minute,
I count. How many hailstones
fall at the same time,

how many smells swirl
in the air at once.
As long as your fragrance is in the world,

you are in the world, your fragrance
overflows me, makes me suddenly
sense your hot cheek,

as though the world belongs to me,
as though I feel certain
about belonging.

As long as your fragrance is there
among the many smells, I dream
about an embrace that's hard as hail.

The smell of books

The smell of books, of paper and printer's ink,
I put my nose down in the book, sniff.
Oxygen for lungs and heart, oxygen for the brain,
the good smell hangs in the nostrils.

I love libraries, love reading rooms with books
read by many, the books change owners,
different hands turn the leaves, their traces
are absorbed by the paper, the smell-imprint deposited
on every page. Someone has been here
before me, I am one of many, others have read
and left their marks before it's my turn,
and someone else again after me.

This book smells of waking dreams, this way
books are interrelated, even though
they are far apart in the rack.
They smell like books on other shelves
in other libraries, I note the smell, live
with it as a part of my life,
a moment's illusory cohesion,
but I trust my senses, what
else should I trust.

Book smells are for anyone, just as
books are for anyone who reads them,
and thereby becomes the chosen one,
the reader the writer dreamed of
so as not only to write to herself,
even when the author is gone
books can still breathe in the reader.

Scents and words live on, transform themselves
in others, perhaps in bodies short-circuited in fear
that the joy will cease one day because
nothing is static. There is just an endless beginning,
alphabets, words, characters become roads,
crossroads, blasted roads, bridges, everything.

Rooms of air are breathed in and out again
when the words are mumbled,
they are inhalation and exhalation,
become rhythm, meaning,
sound of blood, whirling dervishes.

Even in libraries in foreign countries
where I haven't been before,
I feel at home,
in a way they also belong to me.

The books' safe odour also comes to greet me there
when I walk in, the books stand on the shelves,
they are waiting for a reader, open, attentive, receptive,
I am in select company.

Sunk down in the chair I move
over the paper's snow-white or yellowed
pages, my gaze moves like a bird
hopping over the grass, I read
and hold my breath, close my eyes and see,
read and think, read and float,
otherwise you don't get anywhere.

There has been prismatic rain

The world consists of a sum of facts,
not all of them explicable,
I have left a house of tears,
a sleepless city in heavy rain,
I stumbled across the doorstep,
find myself now in a garden
I don't know, still confused.

The sun breaks out, I lose my way
along the paths in the strong light,
am slowly anaesthetised in the rose garden,
it's not a fairy tale,
as I have ants in my shoes.

If smells can sparkle,
it is here in the sodden-ness,
sparkle with the rain's colours.

The smells mingle with the air
I breathe in,
so each rib is stretched out
like the string on a bow,
the air swirls deep
down into the lungs, it whips and stars
out into toes and fingers.

Waves of white oblivion roll in,
the white light from oceans' salt,
the white earth, my heart
beats and beats, restlessly,
this is a moment passing through me,
I like the simple life best,
stake all on smelling it, touching it.

The stream of smells from below

Of the planet's more than seven billion
faces no two are identical.
Even though there are similarities,
each stands out
from the billions of others.

Each person is completely their own
with experiences that resemble
others' and yet
have their own distinctive character.

Together with everyone else
each person
is the only one, equipped with
their own mouth, nose, eyes, ears, skin.

Each person is referred to their own sensations,
as I am now
with the sun in my face, June,
and the chill in my back
stop

to bow down
to the earth, where I sowed seeds,
bow to the flowers at my feet
breathe deeply, sniff in the smell, just
as the more than seven billion
like me around the globe
now and then bow
to the earth
to inhale the fragrances that flow
gentle or prickly as pine needles in the nose.

NOTES

The cream from China (141)
The poem includes lines from Sakutarō Hagiwara's 'The Hand Is a Cake' from *Blue Cat* (1923) translated from Japanese to English by Hiroaki Sato.

After showers of bullets in paradise (160)
The poem derives from the attack on the offices of *Charlie Hebdo* in Paris on 7 January 2015, when twelve people died as a result of a shooting.

Attack on Copenhagen (182)
The poem has its origins in the two shootings at the Krudttønden Cultural Centre in Østerbro on 14 February 2015 at a discussion event called 'Art, Blasphemy and Freedom of Expression' and the shooting at the Great Synagogue on Krystalgade on 15 February, as well as the gunman's death after a shoot-out with police in Copenhagen's Nordvest district.